Maira Kalman

Ah-hA to

For Lulu Bodoni Kalman and Alexander Onomatopoeia Kalman

Published by:
Cooper Hewitt, Smithsonian Design Museum
2 East 91st Street
New York, N.Y. 10128

Distributed by:
Skira Rizzoli Publications, Inc.
300 Park Avenue South
New York, NY. 10010
www.RizzoliUSA.com

For Cooper Hewitt, Smithsonian Design Museum
Pamela Horn, Head of Cross-Platform Publishing

Design: Miko McGinty and Anjali Pala

Library of Congress Control Number
2014933718

 Smithsonian Design Museum

ISBN: 978-0-8478-4377-0 (hardcover)

2014 2015 2016 2017 / 10 9 8 7 6 5 4 3 2 1
Printed in China

Zig-Zag

31 Objects from Cooper Hewitt, Smithsonian Design Museum

Maira Kalman
went to the Museum.
She chose objects
from the collection
and made this Book
for you.
Completely for
You.

COOPER HEWITT Skira RIZZOLI

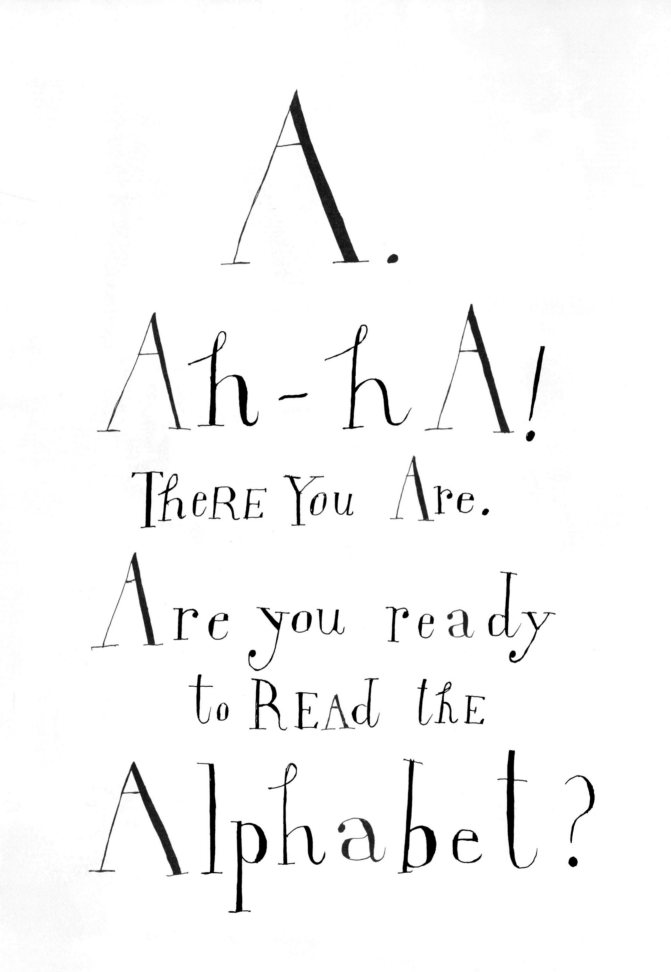

A.

Ah-hA!

THeRE You Are.

Are you ready
to REAd the
Alphabet?

perhaps you should
put on your
ThinKing

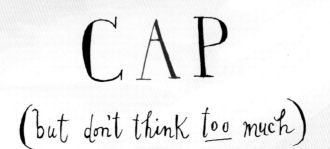

CAP

(but don't think _too_ much)

Big
PROBLEM.

SOMEONE
BROKE
A LOT OF DISHES.
Who?
YOU?

NO, OF COURSE NOT YOU.

(ingo BROKE THEM)
(and put THEM together into A LAMP.)

C.

If YOU Need To
CRY
you should
CRY.

(BUT DON'T CRY ALL DAY LONG —
THERE is much to do.)

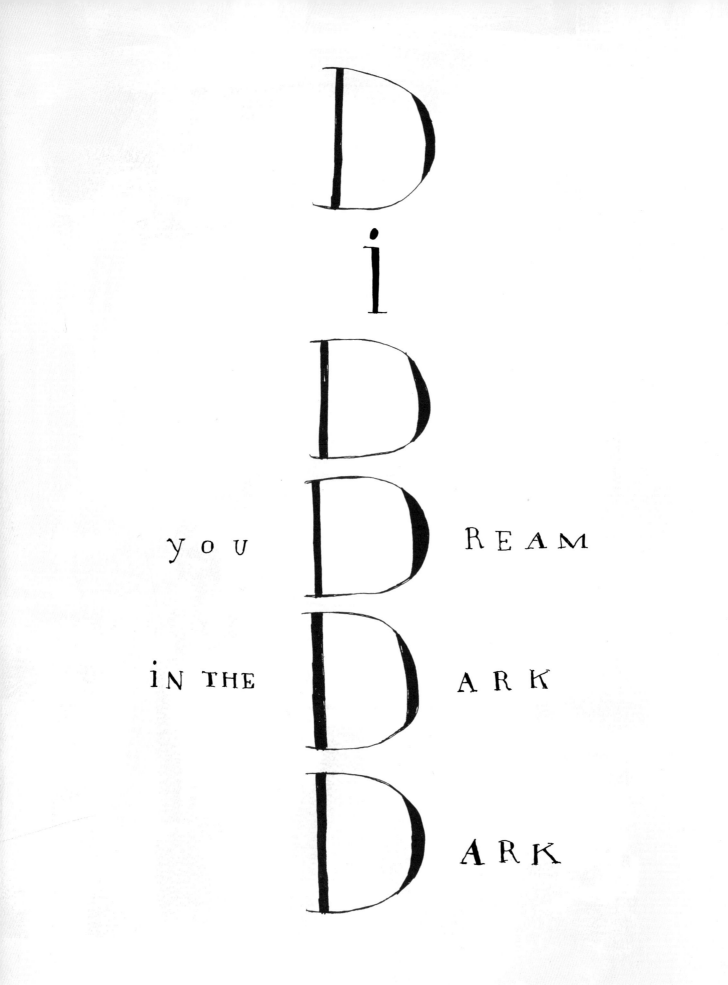

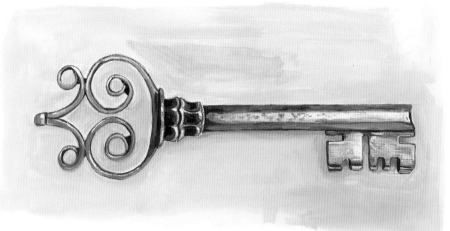

of A
dainty
MAGIC
KEY

or A
DAShing
Rabbit

OR A
StairCASe going
UP into NoWHERE?

E.

(EXCEPT FOR <u>YOUR</u> DOG)

This is the cutest dog on

EARTH.

with

The

Cutest EYEBRows

on

EARTH.

"I Really am Extremely cute."

F.

The hat on this woman From FRANCe is FLUFFY and FROTHY and FANTAStic and FunnY.

G.

Good for you.
You can tell Time.
Goodness Gracious,
What Time is it?
Do we need to GO
somewhere?

(Are We Late?)

H. This is not a Hippo.

1515

RHINOCERVS

This is A RHINOCEROS.

1.

An

itsy-

bitsy

nail.

J.

Just because
you don't like
to comb
your hair,
that doesn't mean
you should
throw out
Your
COMB.

That would be JUST NOT RIGHT.

K.

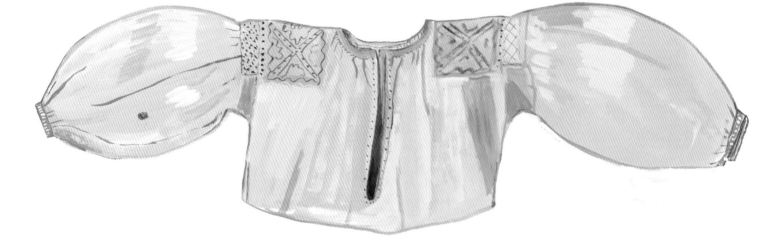

Keep your
shirt on And
Please be Kind.

And walk the dog.

L. if you Lose a button, well, you have to get another one.

Luckily, that is not hard.

M.

Maybe

you will

Memorize

this

Magnificent

Multiplication Table.

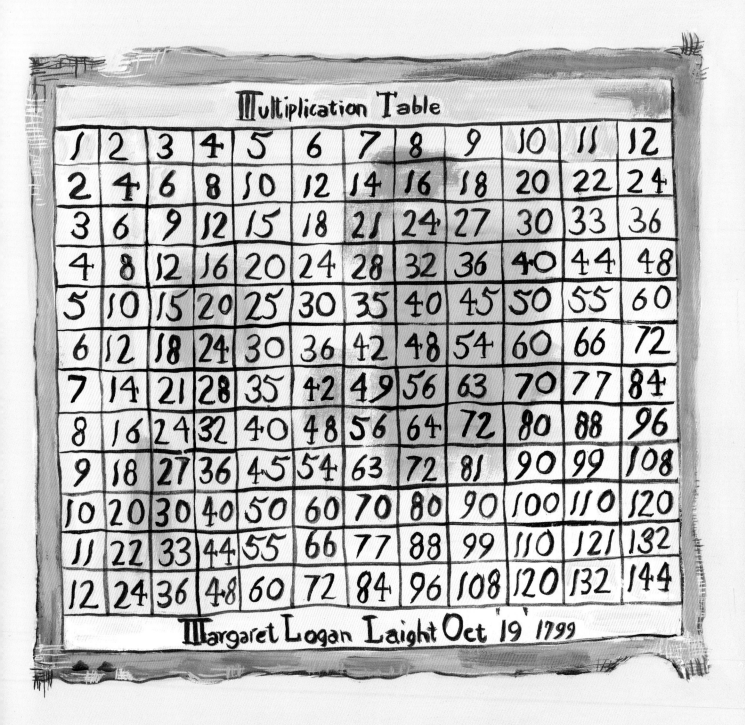

(OR MAYBE YOU WON'T.)

NOW

might be a Good Time
to go to the bathroom.

No worries.

We will wait

for you.

NOT A PROBLEM.

P.

A LONG Time AGO, WOMEN Didn't have

Pockets
in their clothes. WHAT?

Q.

Quite the TOASTER.
(By the way, mind your P's and Q's.)

R. don't Run with Scissors.

(EVEN IF YOU ARE A RABBIT).

 S.

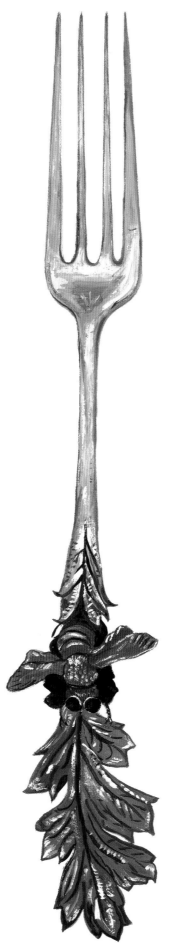

 So,

it might
be time
for a
SNACK.
(Some toast perhaps?)

Sit down

on
A
chair.

MAKE YOURSELF COMFORTABLE

(iF you can).

T.

TERRIBLE
NEWS!

THE toaster
on the Q page
BURNT the TOAST!

You CAN Eat SOME fruit insteAd and

drink Some ginger tea.

U.

When you are standing
under raindrops, put up an
UMBRELLA.

V.

it is VERY very VERY VERY (very) nice to snuggle.

X.

Be

E

tra

CAREFUL
AROUND
MATCHES.
EXTRA!

Dance. Run. Smell flowers. JUMP
for joy. Laugh. CRY. BE mean. Be Kind.
Eat toast. Be cozy. And be foREVER
YOUNG.

Z i g
z a g

life is
NOT a
straight
line.
Life is a
Zig
Zag.

A little forth
A little back
as you
ZOOM
Along.

(Good luck to you.)

Oops!

WE LEFT OUT

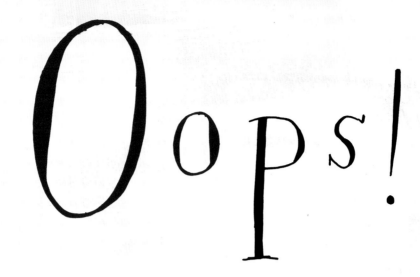

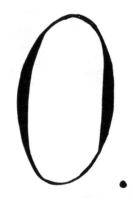

O.

I also make mistakes.

Oh well.
We all make mistakes.
Yesterday I wore
two different socks.
No big deal.

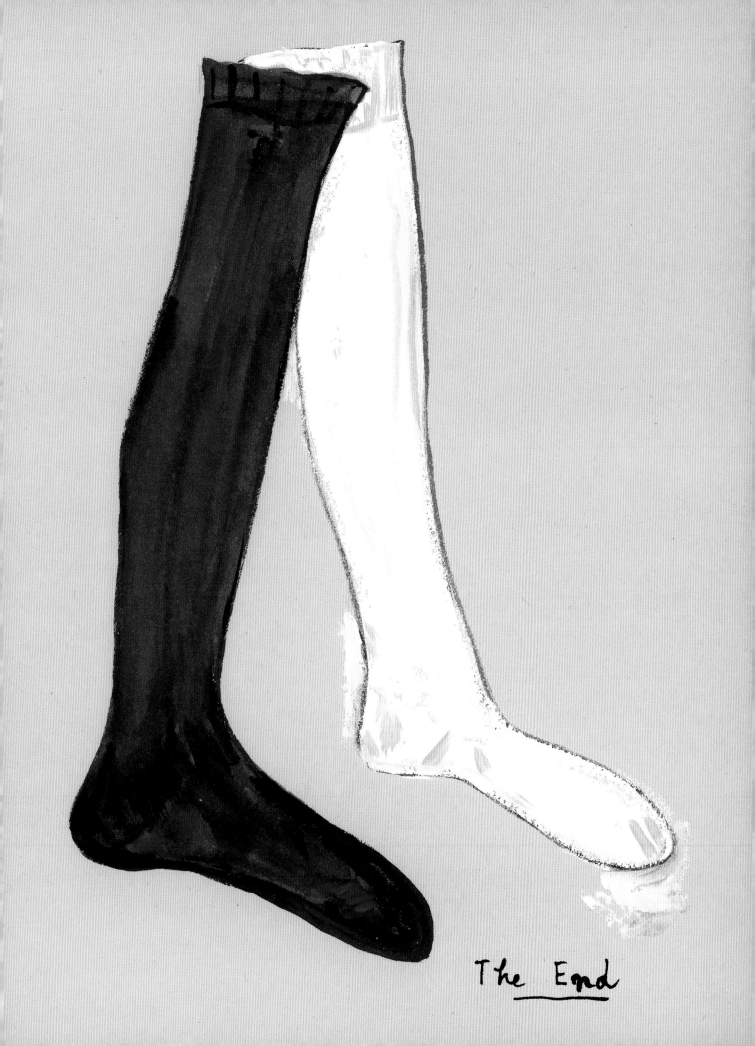

The End

Index of Objects

A.
Cap, Egypt, late 13th or early 14th century; Quilted and embroidered silk with gilded parchment; Gift, Anonymous Donor; 1949-64-7; MF

B.
Hanging lamp, Porca Miseria!, 2000; Ingo Maurer (German, born 1932), manufactured by Ingo Maurer GmbM (Germany); Porcelain, stainless steel, metal, halogen light source; Gift, Peter Norton; 2010-16-1; EM

C.
Medallion, Egypt, 5th–7th century; Wool slit tapestry; Gift, John Pierpont Morgan; 1902-1-72; AG

D.
Key, Italy or Spain, 1770–1810; Wrought, cast, and cut-out steel; Gift, Anonymous Donor; 1952-161-37; MF

D.
Figure, Rabbit, about 1920; Royal Copenhagen Porcelain Manufactory (Denmark); Glazed porcelain; Gift, Mrs. John Innes Kane; 1926-37-210; MF

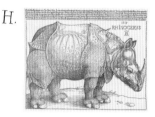

D.
Staircase model, France, about 1820–40; Pearwood, walnut; Gift, Eugene V. and Clare E. Thaw; 2007-45-21; MF

E.
Figure of a poodle, England, 1820–40; Glazed earthenware; Gift, Wendy Vanderbilt Lehman; 1992-5-21; MF

F.
Postcard, A Travers la Normandie: Coiffes et Costumes anciens, about 1909; Paul Bunel (French, 1882–1918); Printed card with hand coloring; Courtesy of the Smithsonian Institution Libraries; DC

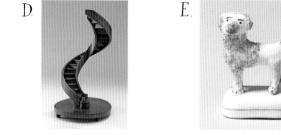

G.
Alarm clock, Big Ben, 1939; Henry Dreyfuss (American, 1904–1972); Manufactured by Westclox (USA); Enameled metal, brass, blued steel hands; Gift, Henry Dreyfuss; 1972-88-185; EM

H.
Print, The Rhinoceros, 1515; Albrecht Dürer (German, 1471–1528); Woodcut on laid paper; Gift, Leo Wallerstein; 1950-5-24; MF

I.
Nail, probably Europe, 1700–1800; Silvered metal; Gift, Unknown Donor; n-a-710; MF

J.
Comb, probably Middle East or North Africa, 19th century; Carved wood; Gift, Kirkor Minassian; 1921-29-25; MF

K.
Blouse, Spain, 18th century; Linen with embroidery and cutwork; Museum purchase, gift of Paul Tuckerman; 1942-28-3; MF

K.
Tile, Alcora, Spain, late 18th–early 19th century; Glazed earthenware (high fired decoration); Gift, Eleanor and Sarah Hewitt; 1920-15-15; MF

L.
Button, possibly Italy, 1890–1925; Enameled and brass-plated cast textured metal; Bequest, Julia Hutchins Wolcott; 1959-66-335; MF

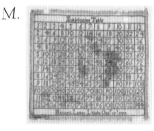

M.
Multiplication table sampler, 1799; Embroidered by Margaret Logan Laight (American); Wool embroidered in silk cross stitch; Gift, Myra and William H. Mathers; 2003-14-2; MF

N.
Toilet (MK)

O.

Pair of stockings, France, 1850–1900; Knitted silk; Gift, Mrs. William P. Treadwell; 1916-33-205-a,b; MF

P.

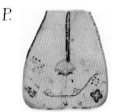

Woman's pocket, USA, 18th century; Linen and cotton, with wool embroidery; Gift, Roxa Wright; 1957-105-1; MF

Q.

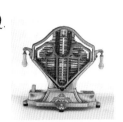

Toaster, Universal, 1920; Manufactured by Landers Frary & Clark (New Britain, Connecticut, USA); Metal, plastic; Purchase, Decorative Arts Association Acquisition Fund; 1993-150-40; MF

R.

Print, Tailleur d'Habits, outils, from *Diderot's Encyclopaedia*, 1763; Designed by J. R. Lucotte (French, 1750–1784), engraved by Robert Bénard (French); Engraving on white paper; Gift, Mrs. George A. Kubler; 1949-152-190; MF

S.

Dessert fork, Paris, France, about 1890; Manufactured by C. V. Gibert (French); Cast and chased silver, gilt silver; Purchase, Smithsonian Institution Collections Acquisition Program, Decorative Arts Association Acquisition, and Sarah Cooper-Hewitt Funds; 1996-56-2; AG

S.

Stool, Puffo, about 1970; Gruppo Strum (Giorgio Ceretti, Pietro Derossi, Riccardo Rosso), manufactured by Gufram s.r.l. (Italy); Polyurethane foam, Guflac® paint; The Linda and Irwin R. Berman Stool Collection; 2008-32-8; MF

S.

Chair, Spun, 2010; Thomas Heatherwick (England, born 1970), manufactured by Magis S.p.A. (Italy), produced by Herman Miller Furniture Company (Zeeland, Michigan, USA); Rotationally molded polyethylene; Gift, Herman Miller, Inc., 2012-18-1; EM

T.

Cup and saucer, Kilta, 1952; Kaj Franck (Finnish, 1911–1989), manufactured by Arabia (Finland); Glazed earthenware; Gift, Harry Blomster; 1985-55-9-a,b; EM

U.

Tile, about 1760; Michael Edkins (English, 1734–1811), Joseph Fowler Factory (Bristol, England); Tin-enameled earthenware, underglaze manganese, overglaze white slip decoration; Purchase, Friends of the Museum Fund; 1938-12-2; EM

V.

Salt and pepper shakers, Town and Country, 1946; Eva S. Zeisel (American, born Hungary, 1906–2011), Red Wing Pottery (Red Wing, Minnesota, USA); Glazed earthenware, cork; Purchase, Charles E. Sampson Memorial Fund; 2000-24-1-a,b, 2a,b; MF

W.

Slippers, USA, 1889; Soldered Tin; Gift, Anonymous Donor; 1937-45-4-a,b; MF

X.

Friction matches, probably USA, late 19th–early 20th century; Sulfur-tipped cut wood; Gift, Stephen W. Brener and Carol B. Brener, 1980-14-1413-a/g; MF

X.

Matchsafe, Cawston Ostrich Farm, South Pasadena, California, about 1900; Whitehead & Hoag Company (Newark, New Jersey, USA); Nickel-plated metal, printed celluloid; Gift, Stephen W. Brener and Carol B. Brener; 1978-146-68; MF

Y.

Square, Boy and Girl, 1947; André Derain (French, 1880–1954), Ascher Squares (London, England); Printed silk; Gift, Cooper Union Art School; 1950-143-8; MF

Z.

Chair, Zig-Zag, Netherlands, about 1934; Gerrit Rietveld (Dutch, 1888–1964); Painted elm; Purchase, Decorative Arts Association Acquisition Fund; 1994-60-1; DK

Rialto Bridge Birdcage, Venice, Italy, late 19th–early 20th century; Painted wood, metal wire, metal; Gift, Eleanor and Sarah Hewitt; 1916-19-14; MF

There were
TWO
sisters.

Nellie

and SALLY
HEWITT

They loved to sing and dance.
They were just a little bit wild.
A little bit.
They had sharp eyes. The
kind of eyes that really LOOK
at things.
One day they decided to collect
the things they loved,
and create a museum.
And they really did it.
Which is a lesson to be learned.
If you have a good idea- DO iT.

One of the first things they collected was this Bird Cage.
(where is the bird?)